yellow

yellow
the verses of HURTING & HEALING

Written & illustrated by
Urja joshi

Anecdote
PUBLISHING HOUSE
For the love of quality reading!

Anecdote Publishing House
2nd Floor 2/15 Lane no. 2 Ansari Road,
Daryaganj-110002

Published by Anecdote Publishing House
Copyright © Urja joshi

Updated Edition 2024

ISBN 978-81-963155-4-2

MRP ₹ 350

All Rights Reserved.
No part of this publication may be reproduced, stored in a retrieval system, or transmitted in any form, or by any means—electronic, mechanical, photocopying, recording or otherwise—without the prior permission of the publisher. Opinions expressed in it are the author's own. The publisher is in no way responsible for these.

Book Promoted and Marketed by Champ Readers Pvt. Ltd.
Edited by Mansi Narula Kashyap
Cover design by Nabanita Das
Layout by Graphic Tailor
Printed by Thomson Press (India) Ltd, New Delhi

Contents

Who are *mohi & kabir*?
(prologue)   vii

mohi.
(the verses of hurting)   1

kabir.
(the verses of healing)   94

Acknowledgements.   194

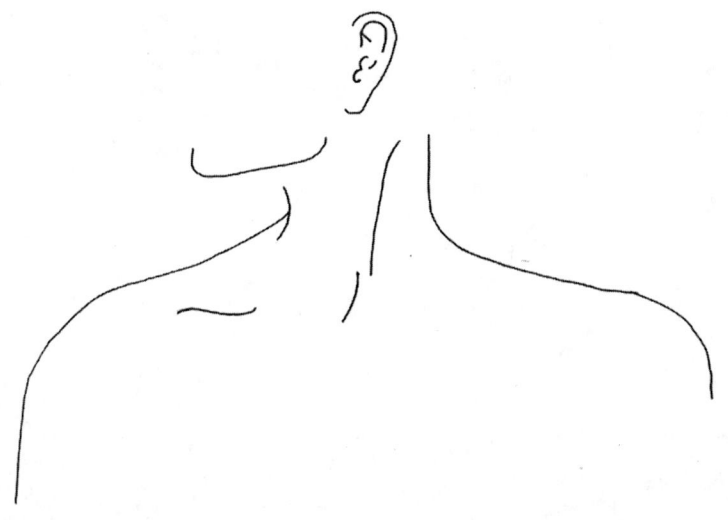

Prologue

who are mohi & kabir?

Just like, there is darkness to every moon, the ray of hope to the most hopeless, the sun of morning to every night, the calm to every chaos, the love you find after the heartbreak, the peace to your anxiety, the blessings that come after sincere prayers & the answers to the most mindbending questions, there is always a mohi to a Kabir.

Much like how there is darkness accompanying every moon, a ray of hope amidst the most hopeless moments, the morning sun following every night, a sense of calm in the midst of chaos, love discovered after heartbreak, peace soothing your anxiety, blessings received after sincere prayers, and answers to the most perplexing questions, there is always a Kabir for every Mohi.

They co exist together, they are worlds apart, yet they find each other and create a beautiful story. Mohi is the dark night, she is hurt, sleepless at night, injured, betrayed, the seeker. Mohi is everyone who has an overthinking mind, a hurt heart, a deep soul, a careful tongue, and a very heavy past, that they carry with them everywhere they go. She is a phase, a term given to all those who feel like her, who are on the same page as her.

Mohi is my ode to all of us, because we all have our bad days. Mohi is us when we can not believe that there ever will be a good day, but after the greatest storm when we go to the same place to pick the pieces back and look at the destruction that has been caused so that we can heal. It is our stronger self, Kabir, who comes to save us. He is the one who knows that it is best to let go of someone if you deserve the best. Kabir believes in the sunrises and better tomorrows. He is the revival and the recovering. Kabir is the calmness that exists in a monk's mind, a healed heart with the ability to spread love in the world. Kabir is my ode to all those who carry their past traumas and griefs so well that they make it look effortless and easy. Kabir is for those who get up after every storm, dust off their knees and get ready for another day. He is the pursuit that Mohi seeks, embodying everything that Mohi aspires to become.

If Mohi is the hurting then Kabir is the healing. They are born for each other. There is no Mohi without kabir and no kabir without Mohi.

The healing will always come after the hurting. Yellow is a gift for all of us and I can't wait for you to unwrap it.

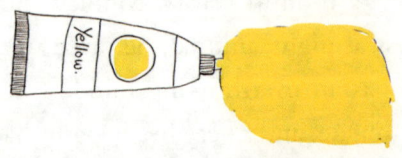

mohi
(the verses of hurting.)

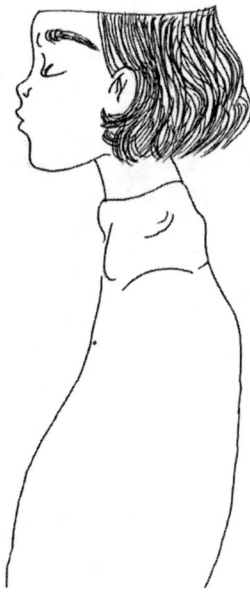

I am the abused,
And
I am the hurt,
I am
The maltreated
The punished,
and
the seeker.
-ohi

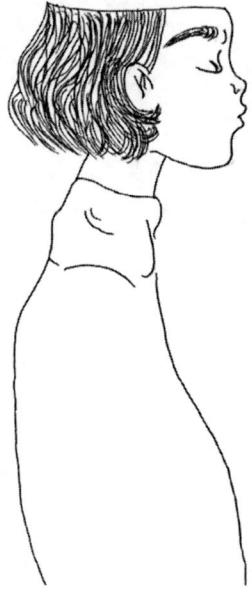

When
the person I love Bid me farewell,
We exchanged some gifts. I gave him,
A part of mine To take with him.
and
He gave me,
Some beautiful memories
To remember forever.

WhenI hold the pen and paper
I wander in my thoughts
What should I write about today?
I look down and
my hands are already writing about you.

    -Sometimes I write about you with my eyes closed.

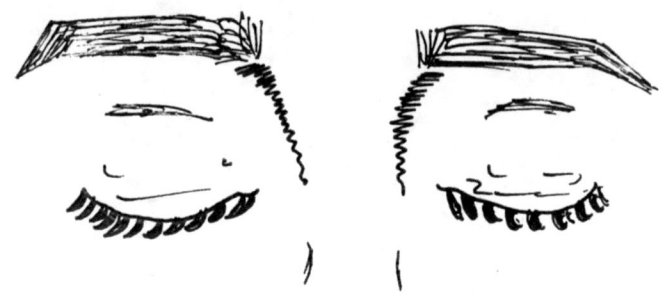

I crave,
Not someone greater than you
Nor do I crave someone lesser
I want you,
So do not fool yourself
By telling me
That I deserve better
Because who said?
I want better.

I have been told that I deserve better
But to be with you
I settle for less.

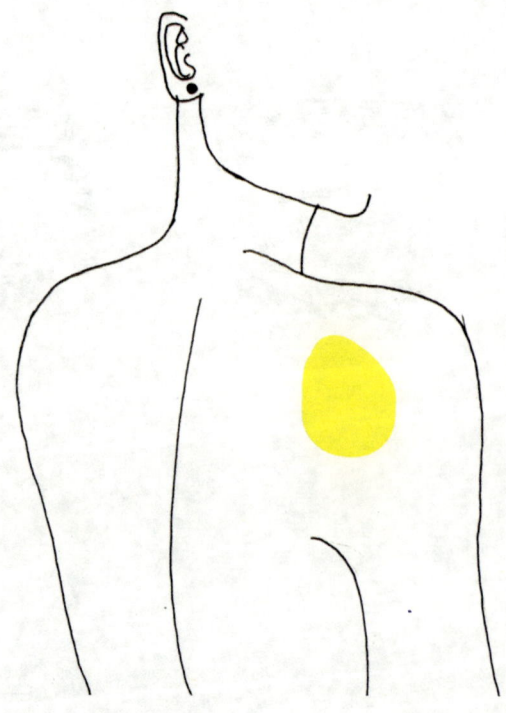

What sort of love is that?
Which can only be spoken of
And not shown?
What sort of love is that?
Which exists
only in your words
And not in
your actions?

Do not talk about faith to me
I grew up believing
That
I am not pretty
But
the day he told me,
He thinks I am beautiful
I believed it
In a second.
Every word he spoke
Sounded like
The truest thing
I have ever heard.

All the trust that I gathered,
My trust in love
And my trust in forever,
My trust in loyalty
And my trust in promises,
My trust in happy endings,
Followed by,
my trust in myself bit by bit
I put all of that trust in you.
And now you have left
With all the trust
That I have ever had.

>*-trust issues*
>*No trust left to put in others*

Whether we are
8 Or 18
40 or 80
We all understand love.
Because age is for the body
Your heart never grows,
It always knew
How to love.
It will die knowing
How to love.

-Too young or too old to love?

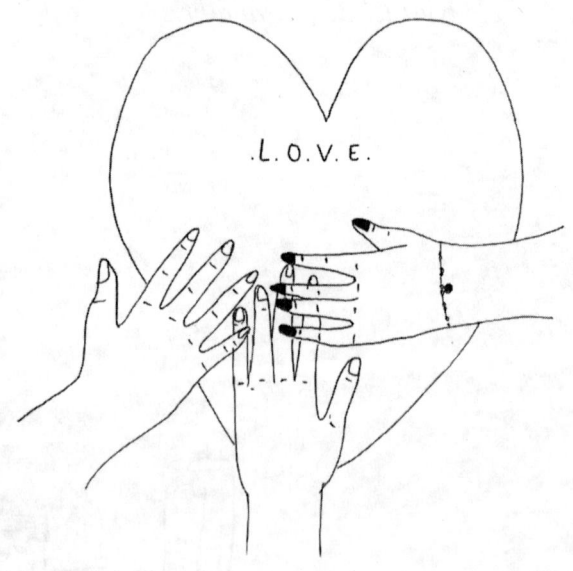

Absence of him Is like
An absurd absence.
It is, as if
When a part of you Goes missing.
As if
someone has chiseled
Out my hands
And I have not functioned
Normally ever since

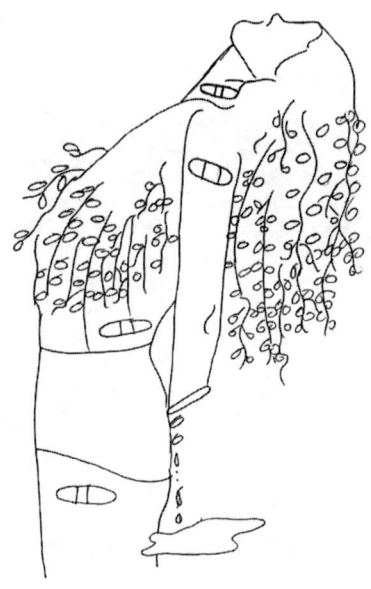

It was not
such a hard pill
To swallow When he said
He doesn't love me anymore
As if
I was not noticing that
His hands have
Been somewhere else.
Lately.

    -Sensed it before you confessed

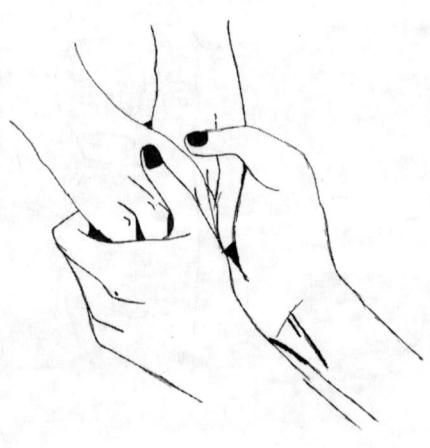

I listen to you
Describing her
As if she is the greatest art you have ever seen.
But have you
Ever overheard conversations
That I have with my friends?
Did you ever listen
The way I talk about you?

   -when it is one sided.

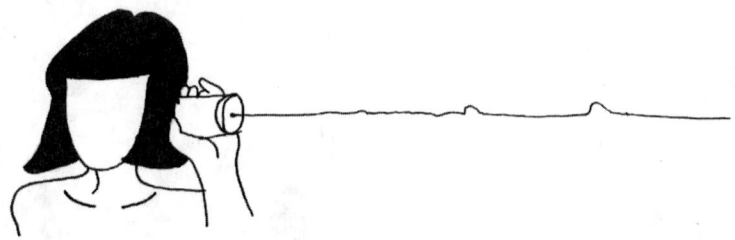

Whenever you have said
That I don't understand you
I tried my best
Pulled my hair and slapped myself
But
how do I tell you
I don't understand, me either?
The love
I have never tasted myself
How am I supposed
to serve it
To you?

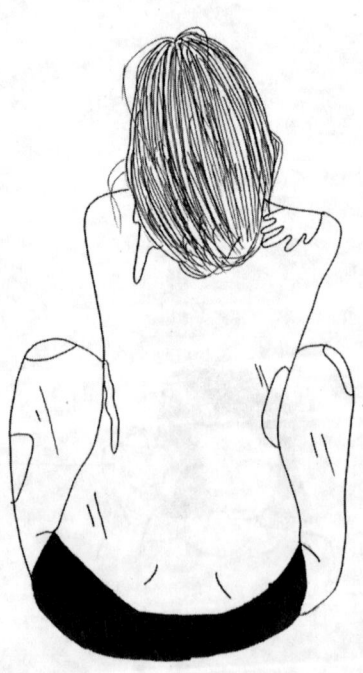

You think you are ready
For the loss
You think
you are preparing
Your mind
and
your heart And your body
For their leaving in advance
But you can not.
When they will leave
you will feel the pain
Despite so many preparations
You will always feel the pain
Because love does not work like this.

-Of course it is going to hurt.

Yellow

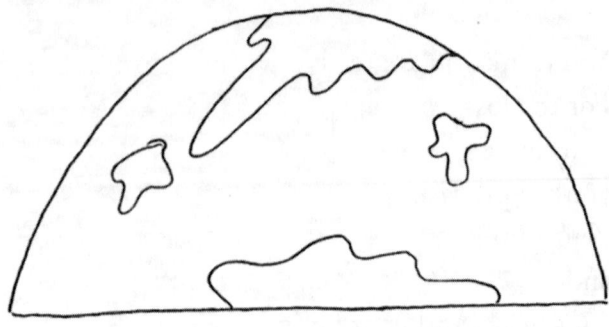

And
I will be always so grateful that
Our paths crossed with each other's
in this lifetime
there is so much of the world
I will never experience
But
the little part
I witnessed,
had you in it
Could I be any luckier?

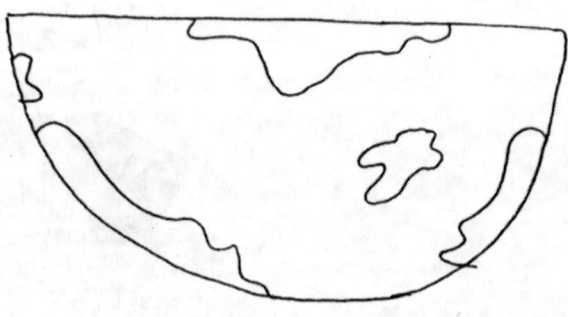

My hands are automatic
With your name
I know how to spell you
With my eyes closed
And so is my tongue
Even when I am talking
To people I have known
For years
your name
Slips out
As if a reflex.
It's like
I have only known you the best
And no one else.

I sat in front of mirror today
Looked at my short hair,
The length was your favorite
Dyed in blue,
Your favourite hair color on women
Looked at my trimmed nails
Because you found long
Acrylics-nasty.
Looked at the short dress
I was wearing
Because the more skin I showed
The more appealing I looked to you.
From head to toe
I was yours
And your ideas of a perfect woman.
I was so yours that
I was never mine.
So now that
You have left
The first thing I should do
Is to get rid
Of these lies
Because they never made me
Perfect enough
For you
To stay.

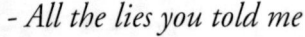

- All the lies you told me

You fall for the lust
And call it love.
And then
The lust Betrays you
And you blame
The love.

    - The thin line we cross every time.

If you wonder What it is like
To keep only
The good parts of someone?
Then
Let me explain
 It to you
 It is simple
It is like
Not really being a writer
But just writing about them
Writing about only the good in them
And not the pain they
Brought with them.

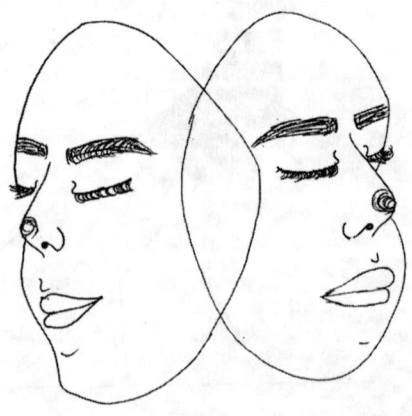

So here I sit
Today
In the garden of love
Writing you
Love letters,
in every language,
that you can speak
or understand
So that you don't have an excuse
to not read.

-Not leaving a chance for them to not accept your love.

How naïve can I be?
The love which brought
Self doubts
And harm with it,
Was of course
Not mine
To keep.
My love is
Supposed to make
Great things happen.
My love is supposed to
Move the mountains.

   -The Red flags

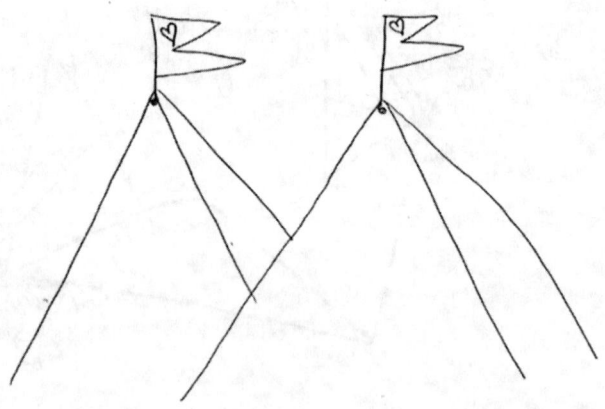

They gaze into my eyes, as though trying to perceive the turmoil within. They witness my tears and reassure me that things will improve. They claim to empathise with my emotions, yet pass judgement on others in similar situations. Now, take my hand and let me know if you can grasp the depth of despair I'm experiencing at this moment. Hug me and tell me if my struggle of getting out of my room, every morning, gets to you. Open your ears and tell me if you can hear the multitude of insecurities and thoughts that plague my mind, eroding my self-esteem day by day. Extend your hand and tell me if you can hold your heart like I hold mine, with courage and grit with endless hopes that maybe tomorrow is different. See through your eyes and tell me if you can notice the dark eyes of mine struggling to sleep every time.

Ask your heart, if she can feel the pain of mine, which is broken and trying to find meaning in every breath I take. And If your body does not respond to all of these questions, you shall know how much of a privilege it is to have support of yourself and how not okay it is to bring those people down, who don't have this.

—From those who are depressed
To those who aren't.

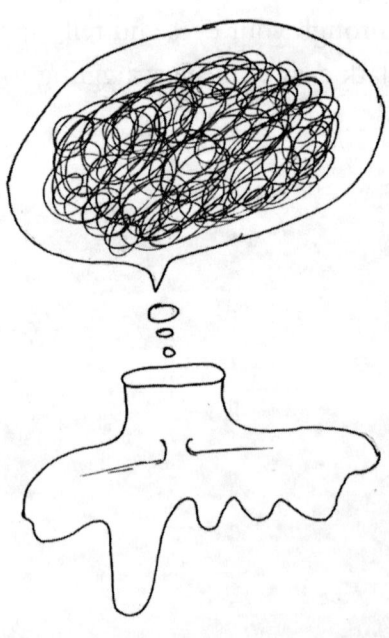

If I say
I am at home
I am either In your arms
Or
In a sunflower garden.

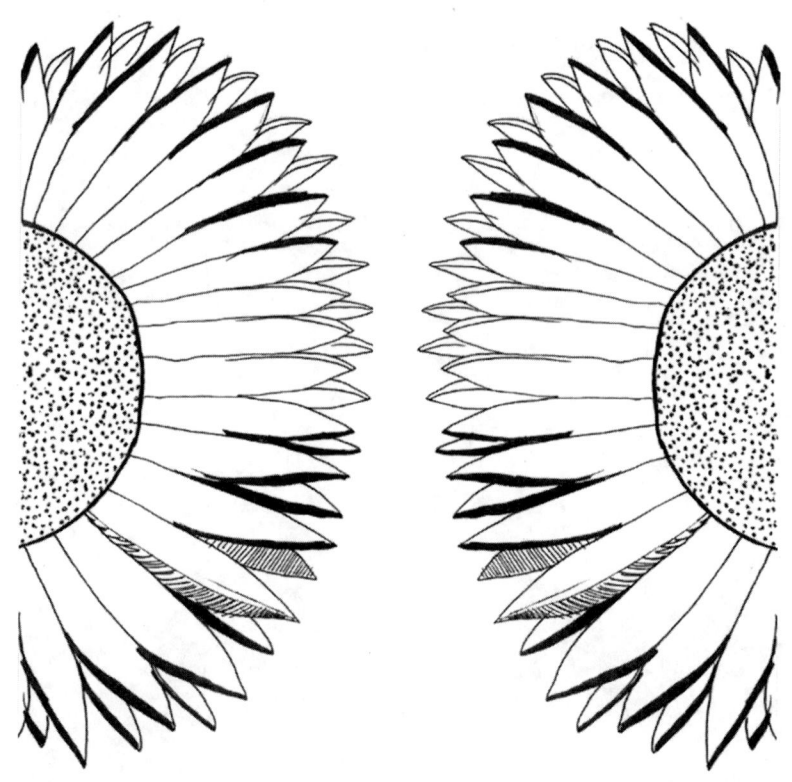

Out of many lessons
That I learnt
From you,
The greatest was
of appreciation.
to stop sometimes
and appreciate
someone's presence,
so enough,
that they never have to leave.

*—Sometimes we don't
appreciate enough*

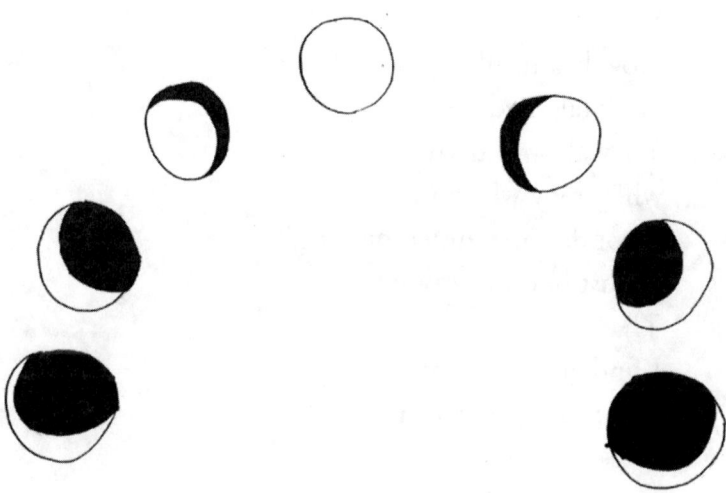

Great love
Comes in your life
Only for
once
But the illusion
That it has come, finally,
Comes
more than that.

    −The mistake of " the one"

So pretty!
How beautiful!
How talented,
They all would say,
when they witness me
I wonder how much hatred
I must have for myself
That
I find all these praises
way too much for me.

    —Self hate

You run
your fingers
across my hair
And put me to sleep
As if
only to pretend
That you love me
till my eyes are open
to see it.
I deserve a kiss
on the forehead,
even if I am not
Conscious enough to feel it.
I deserve the love
Even if I am asleep

—*Secret affection*

People will call you
Their home.
But
do not fall for it
Because they
Abandon homes
They are the
Travelers.
And
you will have to just
Wait for them
To come back.
While they will be
Busy
exploring the world.

    –Home.

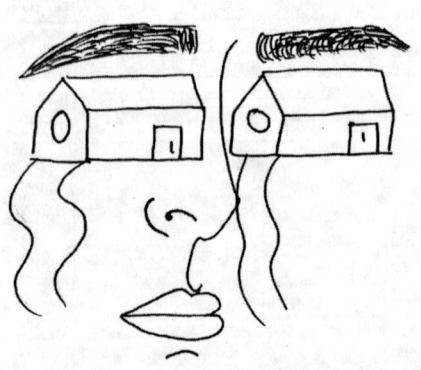

If I ever wrote the most beautiful Letter
I will never conclude it By writing
"yours"
At the end
I will just put
"mine"
As the last word.
Because I belong to me,
And the more I say
I am yours
The more
I take away me
From me.

    —My contribution in being myself

You open the door
To enter the home
and get rid of clothes,
you were wearing
And then
you cry your eyes out
You close the doors,
The windows
That bring the
 air of happiness through them
and double lock them
You make yourself disappear
and when the moon becomes the sun,
9pm becomes 9am
You put back your fake smile
Prepping for the world
With no intentions
of being happy.

*—When was the last time you
got happy, for real?*

When the waves
of the ocean
hit the shore
It takes some of the sand with it
And leaves behind some.
You look
at what is left behind
But
you never see
what has been washed away
You stand there
what they have left for you
But you never take a moment to reflect
What they took away with them
It's your permanent pain and tears.

—all that he packed, when he left

If
it was
the love that hurt you
Then
it shall be love,
who will do the healing.
But
How dumb of you
To expect
the love
Of hurting and healing,
Both,
From the same person?
    —They can not be the illness and the medicine both.

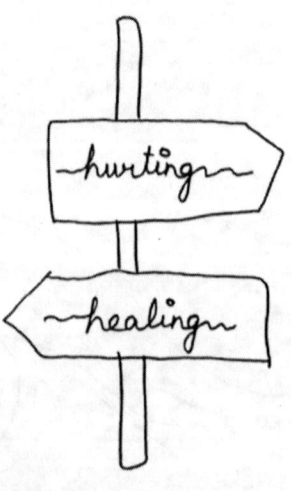

Maybe
Our hearts
Shatter into
Millions of pieces
So that
We can look at them
And realize
That we never gave
Even the tiniest of those pieces
To ourselves.

Yellow

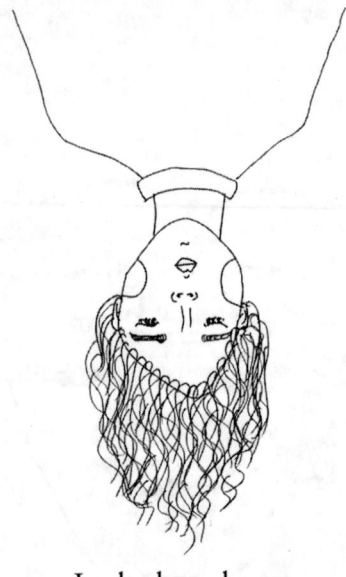

I asked my heart
I am not sure whether I will reach there or not.
But can you tell me
What will I do on the day
I will let go of this pain?
Will I cry?
Will I never think about him?
Will I forget every beautiful memory
He was a part of?
I want to know.
Every question as if creating a havoc in me
Tell me, I demanded
They say heart knows everything
Then speak up
How will I behave on the day I will let go of him
Will I curse him anymore?
Or will I curse myself?

Tell me.
My heart felt pity for me
As if sympathizing with me
"you will do nothing
You will just sit and
Thank him
For walking out of you
You will thank him
For letting go of the space in your heart
That was meant to be taken by you.
You will thank him for letting you know
that your heart beats for you more
than it beats for anyone else."

All the mornings
and late nights
And all the dusks and dawns
I have only sung love songs
For you.
So loud, with the hope
You would listen
And maybe come back to
Shut me up at least.

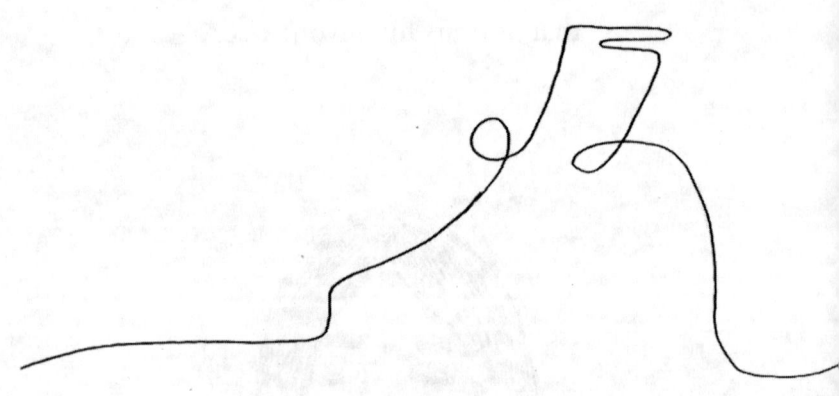

11:11
Make a wish he said
"may the sunflowers
Of happiness and joy
In you
Never wilt."
I prayed.

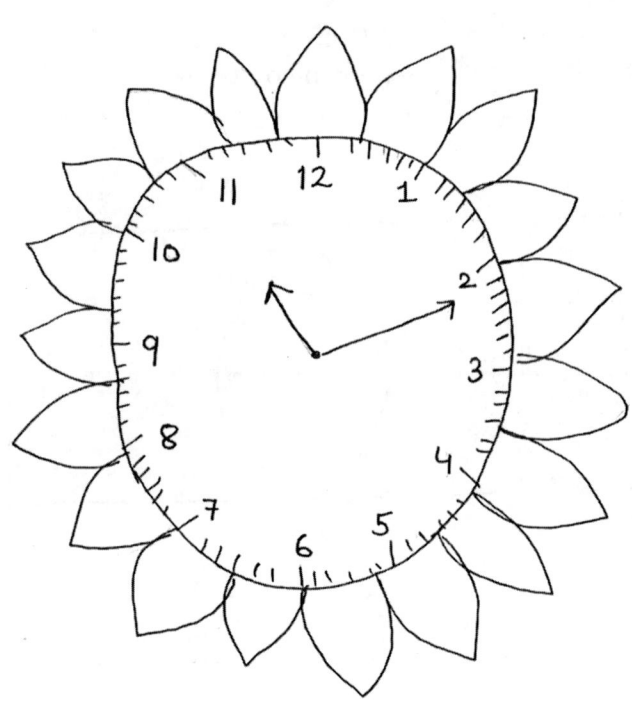

You were like the sea
reflecting the colors
Of everything
Around it.
& here I was
Being befooled like
A sun, who
Thought
That you
Are always
Yellow in color.

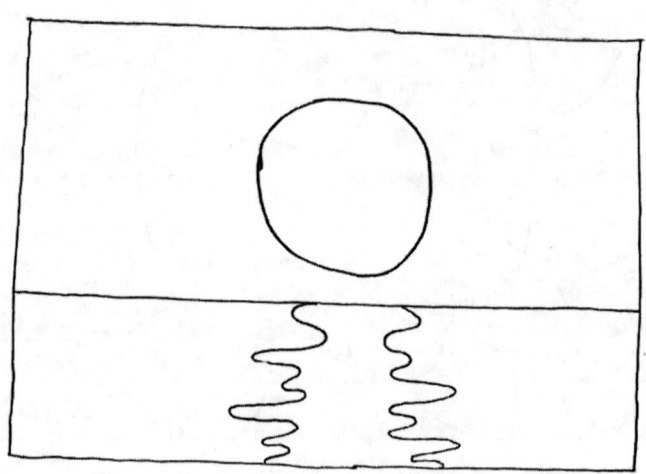

I looked at him and saw
not what he was but
all that he could be
Validated my love for him
More than
I validated
My love for myself
Again my rage evaporated
Again I found a reason to stay

   –forgiving

The apologies
You never made
And yet I gave you.
The gratitude you never
Showed, but i
Still whispered
"you are welcome" for.
The I love yous, you
Never told me and
Yet I reassured you of my love.
The drop
Of care and affection
You never gave, but
All the oceans I offered to you
What sort of love is this?
What do we call it
The things you always took
From me,
But never gave back.

–Give and take

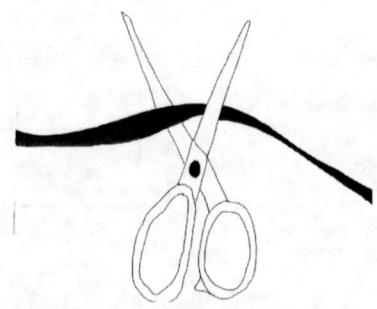

When the moon
asks about you
I gracefully change the topic
Because
I know that
the night is not long
Enough
to let me speak about you
And
the moon can not stay forever to listen.

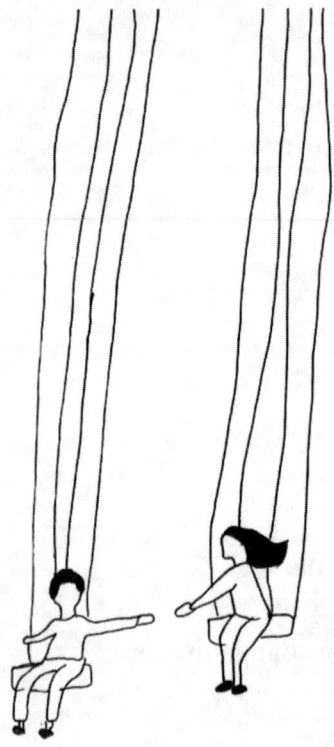

Be it
Day one
Or this day
When I see you
You take my breath away
In Fact you take all my breathes away
It's like
A difficult choice
To make
To choose looking at you
Or
To choose breathing.

Yes,
I still pour tea
in two cups
One for me
and one for him
Only to realize
that he has left
And yesterday is not the same
And also
that one cup is enough.

    —Habit of them, stays longer than them.

When I look in the mirror
Smiling,
at the woman
looking back into my eyes.
I see her scars,
I see her wounds,
Which have no intentions of healing.
I look at her heart,
as if it has been
Ripped out and wearied
"oh!" comes out of my mouth,
"so love did this to you"
and
She replies back
Love is not the one to be criticised
 When it's your fault
How dare you love someone else more than Me.
I stand like a victim in the court
Who is guilty
and who has no answers

—confrontations

Maybe
The reason that
They let go
of you, is
Because you are
So good
That they don't know
What to do with you.

Yellow

And
if you've to impress me
Do not compliment
my skin deep beauty
Say that it's my brain and
the way I see the world
which moves you.

I gave
the acceptance
To your imperfections
I never even
Gave to myself.
My heart
And
my body
My soul
And
my mind
they are jealous of you
 in ways
you can not think of.

 —*My scars are ugly but I find yours beautiful.*

How amazing it is
To look at him
And feel
the warmth of sunshine
Yet
the calm of the moonlight all
At once.
it is like
i am witnessing
the entire universe
when I lay my eyes on him.

It was never about
how many times i
told you
"I am fine"
and other funny lies.
it was always about
how often you believed them.

–How are you?

Yellow

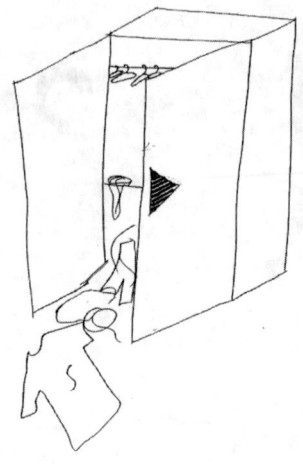

I opened my closet
And
a t shirt of yours
Fell in my feet
As if asking me
Why do I not wear it anymore?
For once,
I thought
of throwing the shirt out
Of my home.
But
I could not
What would I have as an answer?
If you return to me
And ask for it?
I felt so irritated
Because
I was me

Why can't I become
you
So unkind.
I hold onto your t shirt
As if it's everything
You did not
Hold onto
My heart,
Treating it
As if it was nothing.

    —The difference between you and me

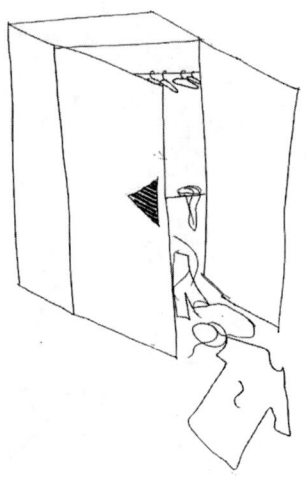

They promise you
and then
They leave you
like the sun leaves the sky
 At the end of every day.
Making it all warm hued
followed by dark night.
They paint you in their colors
 To make sure
The world never forgets that once
 You were in love
And you had a heartbreak.

—Sunsets and heartbreaks

There will be
so many things
I want to say
but I will not
And so many questions
 I would want to ask,
but I will not
A lover in me
still believes
that you understand my silence.

    —Telepathy

I would tell
every stroke of wind
Passing through me
That tell him
I miss him
So did you get the message?
yes?
Then why haven't you replied
No?
why has the nature betrayed me.

My grief ends the day
I realize that
Love is not supposed to be romantic
 It is not an emotion for lovers
It is for all of us
And I deserve it
Too.
The day I realize
Love is not dead
Just because one person
Did not love me back.

And when
I say
I feel good
Do not
Believe my
Smiling face
It is her habit
To hide
And hide.
Till people
Believe it.

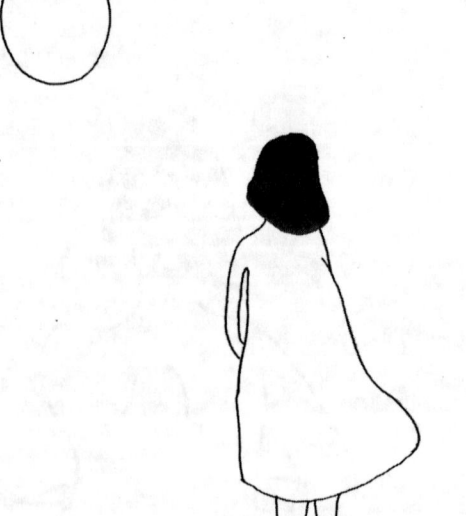

His departure
Was the most
Painful and vibrant
Memory
In my brain.
 I wish
It was 32nd july
 When you
Had to leave.
A date to never come
And
you never to go

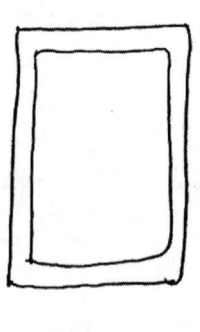

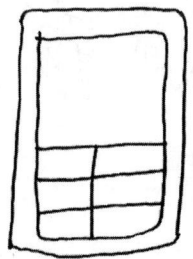

It was
Extraordinary
When I saw you
For the very first time
As if I knew
I will fall in love with you
Not right then
But one day
For sure.

love!

Sometimes I wonder
Why did I even
Confessed
That I loved you
I should have known
When I say
I love you
It's my problem to deal with
What can you
Do
In this?

love!

In this
relationship
Of yours and mine
You were the
One always telling me
What's your favorite
And I was
Always learning them
Practicing them.
I wanted to be you
Or at the least like you
So that you can love me
Like you love yourself.

I can not
Live the
Final moments
Of our story.
I am so scared
So
Do not say
A hopeful goodbye
Do something terribly
Wrong to me
And then leave
So that I can hate on you
For the rest of my life.
So that I can remind myself
That
No!
I don't have to remember you
At all.

My therapist
Kind of had
Her eyebrows raised
When I told her
I don't need the pills
I need him
He is the solution
To my anxiety
Maybe
she realized
I am kinda
Screwed up.

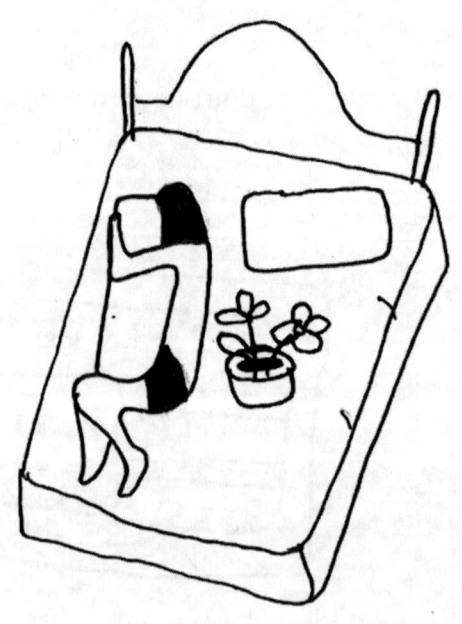

I say
I am over him
And yet
I write
Poems
So obvious that
When he will read
He will know
It's about him.
For he knows
He is the greatest Art
I have ever seen.

Homesick
For you.
A place
I can't return to
because
I know
If I go back
I won't be
Welcomed

△▽△▽△▽△▽ △▽△▽ △▽ △▽ △▽

Of all the things that
Remind me of you
Your imprints
On my skin
Are my favourite.
As if telling the world
I was yours
And
I shall be that,
Forever.

△▽△▽△▽△▽ △▽△▽ △▽ △▽ △▽

To breathe alone
And to sleep with me
To have no one
By my side
Is surely a hard thing to do
But to have you
And then feel Lonely
Is harder.
I know its harder
But still
I choose the harder way.
Because if solitude
Has to hit me anyway
Then let it hit me
When you are here.

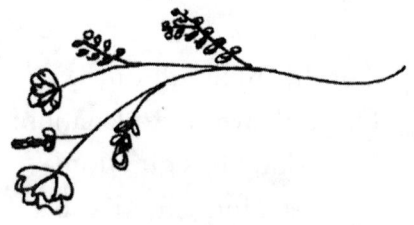

How am I
Supposed to heal
if I keep
Cursing him
and blaming him
For the hurt.
That
I caused to myself.
I have to thank him.
I don't have to
Lose my kindness
I have to lose my Pain.

For the millionth time
You hurt me
And
For the millionth time I ask
"Do you have an explanation?"
Asking this question
Is just a formality I know
I have already
Forgiven you.

It is not too much
To ask for When I say
I am not seeking love
I want
Love to seek me.
I want
Love to come to me
And stand in front of my eyes
Touch me & awaken me
I want love To feel right.

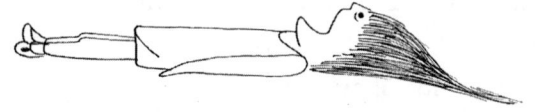

Yellow

Sitting in shower At 3 am
Taking my breathing For granted
Constantly telling
My mind
That it is okay
To be not loved back
It is okay
To not have a life
Which matches to the definition of normal
To not have stable emotions,
It is okay
To have this want of crying all day
It is okay
To not feel motivated,
when you wake up in the morning
But
What is not okay
Is to not
Love myself.
To end all of it
Thinking that
Tomorrow will never change.
It is not okay
To not give your life a chance
To show her good days
To you.

—Suicidal

I check
My wardrobes
The bathrooms,
The kitchen and the hall
I check my body
Looking for something
That you might have
Left by chance
Maybe
An excuse to come back.

–Denial

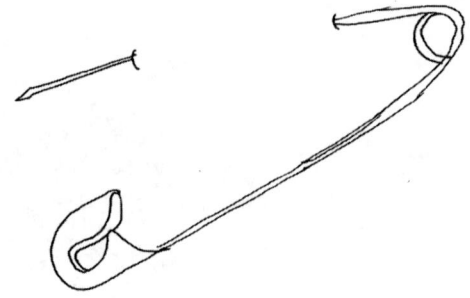

Yellow

I don't remember
Wanting someone
Who would just
Wake up
One day
And tell me
That he doesn't love me anymore.
 Rather
I wanted to have someone
 Who would remind me
 That he loves me
More than the day before.

—A love that never dies

If their cologne
Is not the most aromatic air
Your nose has inhaled.
If their voice
Is not the best music
You have ever heard.
If their eyes
Aren't the deepest
Ocean you have
Ever drowned in.
If you
Don't feel like
Worshipping their entire existence
Because they are
Too good to be true
then
My friend
You still haven't known
What love is.

    –The one

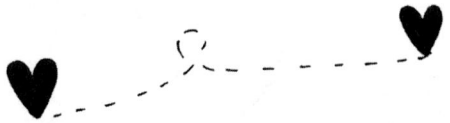

Do not suggest
Me to forget you
I will unlearn you
To an extent
That even if
You stand in front
Of me
I will have to
Put in my best effort
To revive
Your memory
In my head.

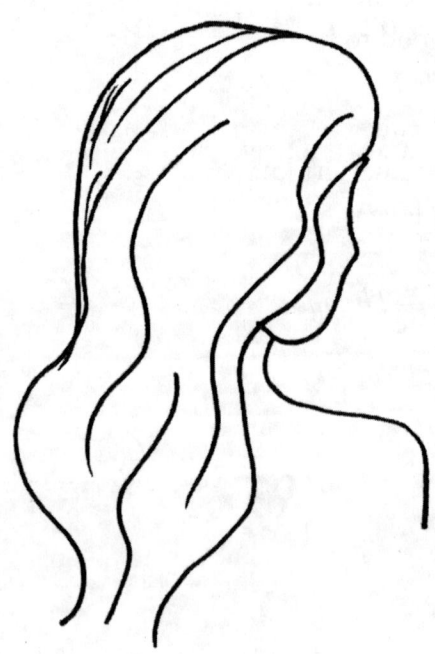

I aspire
To be the kind
Of woman
Around whom
Men are not afraid
To cry.
Other genders
Feel safe around her.
The kind of woman
Who doesn't threaten
Anybody's
Respect & Opinions.
The kind of woman
Who is
Enough
With or without
Someone.

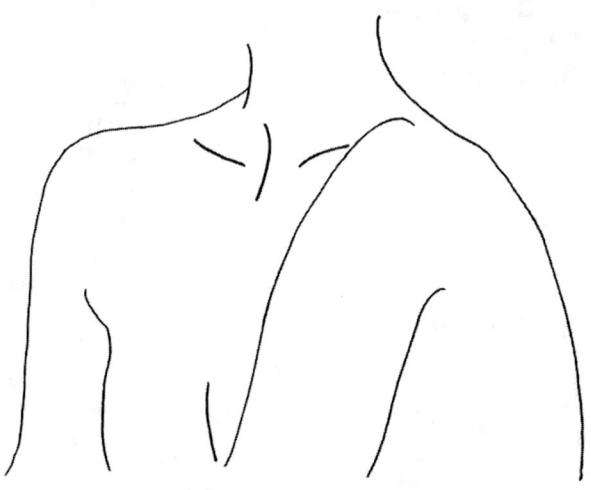

When I undress myself
In Front of mirror
I can see All those
Scars on my body
Which remind me
Of
What it is like
To fall out of love.
But some say
It is okay
So what if
Their touching
Bruises you
So what if It hurts.
Not only the body,
They will damage
The heart as well.
And if I believe them
& I let that happen to me
I am nothing
But a weak woman in love.

—*violence*

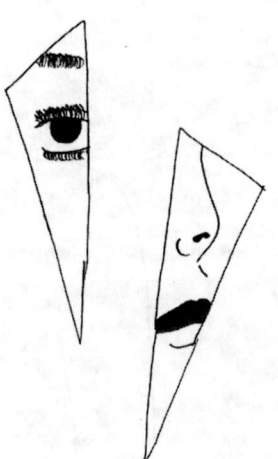

The more
I run towards
You
The more
Far you appear.
like
To know you
Is like
Peeling an onion
It never ends.
A layer
After layer
And also
Lots of tears.

    –He says he is a closed book

I don't know
How to write
Love letters to myself.
I don't know
What to write in it
Shall I apologize to myself
Or confess my love
Or should I
Simply thank myself
Please,
Tell me someone
What exactly
Do we write
In the love letters that
We write to ourselves?

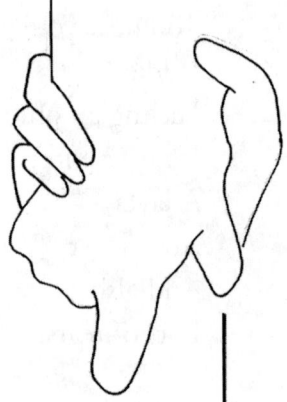

So someone says
Write the letter
As If you are your own lover
 Now it is like
Describing those parts of me
Which take my breath away
My pen would not move Because
I don't know
What is appreciable about me
To write about me
Starts with knowing myself

Now I am sitting here
To explore myself
To teach myself About the way
I see this world.
I practice by speaking
My favourite color
My interests
My favourite foods

And
What a glory To find
That
When I ask myself
What is my favourite color?
I say out loud "black"
But black is not what I like
Black is your favourite

I know you so well
The way you like your coffee
The way you like
Water in the bathtub
When you
Bathe for the second time
But
I don't know anything
About me.
I can love you
But I haven't been taught About
How to love my own self.

   –I don't know me

What is
So hurtworthy
About me?
What is
So permeable
About me
That people
Come in and go out
So effortlessly.

   —Self doubts

I want to
Go back in time
A day before I met you
And tell myself
That
"The person
Who will attract you
And the person who will
Look like love to you
Is not really
What you want to have.
Walk past him
And never make those eye contacts
Even if it kills you,
Don't start that conversation.
 Don't let him
Catch you
When you fall in love.
 If possible
Don't fall at all."

–*Undo*

I could not
Hold my hand
as well as yours
At the same time
So
To be with you
I let go of mine
Now here I am
Neither do I have you
Nor
I have myself.

–lost

Yellow

The moon has the stars
But the sun is lonely.
If you shine
Bright enough
You don't really
Need anyone by your side.
Your love
Makes enough light
For you
And the world.

—For Women who don't have a partner.

What kind of
Audacity I have.
I have never been there for me
And yet
I expect the world
To be there
When I need help
When I need love.

I accept,
That
To be apart
From you
Is to be
Closer
To myself.
And
I am okay
With it.
And even if
I am lying right now
I know
I will be okay with it
One day.

I wish to have so much love in me
That I never have to choose between giving it to them
And keeping it for me.

—Abundance

Why do you want to hold the hand
of someone
Who wants to leave
why do you want to need someone
Who won't need you
In the same way
What's so fascinating about things
Which aren't meant for you.

–questions for myself

On day 1 of being without you
I felt grief twist and turn inside me
But I remembered how
I felt worse in your presence
I felt so unseen
So misunderstood
And so Unlovable
And I didn't even have your absence to blame for it

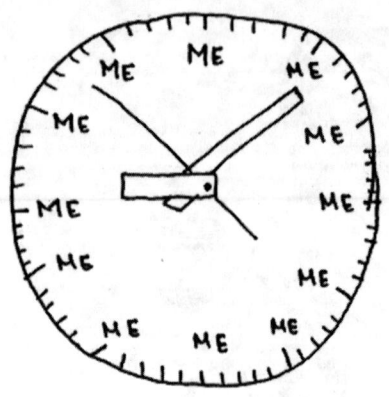

I woke up at a random hour
It was a May night
And I prayed
For me and you to find happiness
It was as if the God himself came to me that day
To answer me
The next thing I remember was
You were gone.
Happiness and togetherness doesn't always end up in the same dish
We did find happiness
But in complete different realities
In two different worlds
Yours was in a world where I didn't exist
And mine was waiting for me
Where I had forgotten about you.

–It happened for a reason

After years of being together
You asked me
What all I've done for you
When I know that everytime
I called you
The love of my life
For a moment
Everything in me
Felt so envious
I heard my mind and heart saying,
"Has she ever talked about us
this way?"
I gave you the love
that I kept hidden from my own self
And you ask
What all have I done?

—After years of abandoning myself
When I finally came home to me
Nothing felt the same.

kabir
(the verses of healing.)

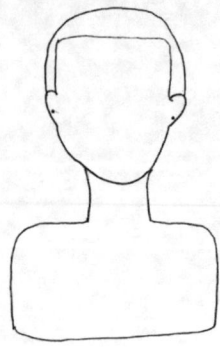

*I am
the revived,
the cured.
And
I am
the healed.
I am
the seeking*

—kabir

Even when I write this
The earth below my feet
Is moving.
A second from my
Bad day is reducing.
That's how I know
It is not forever,
Good or bad
It is not here
For long.

It is okay for me
To cry
and plead
and break
But it shall not be okay
For me
To do that
forever.

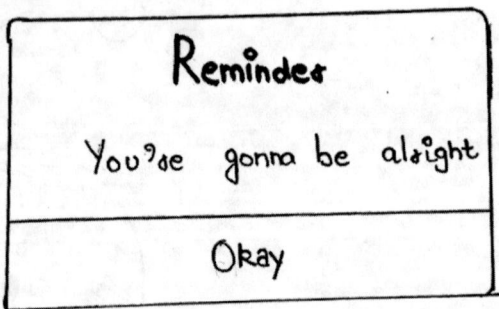

if I feel empty
And I think
Another person can cure
That for me
There is nobody
More wrong
Than me
I need to know that
If I feel empty
Only i can make
Myself full again.

If there is God
In the universe
And stars
He might be smiling
At us
Right now
And laughing at
Our priority list
Which has everything
But
our own names.

And
if the future generations
Ever ask you
Who are women?
Tell them that
Women are everything
That men think they are not

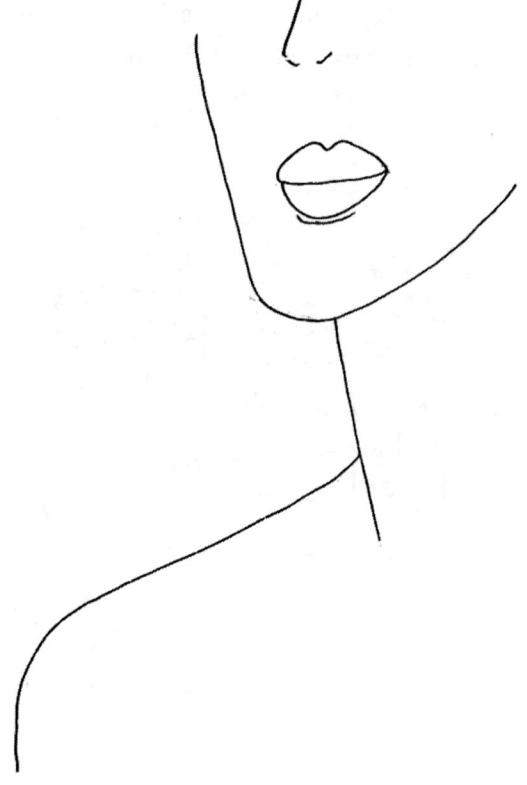

Hug the lonely
Surely do
But also hug
The one you think
Is the strongest
It is a tiring job
To be the one with strength always
To pile up all the insecurities
In a corner of the heart
And telling them to never Find a way to mouth
They need it
The most
Because they don't show it And that's why
They will always need it the most.

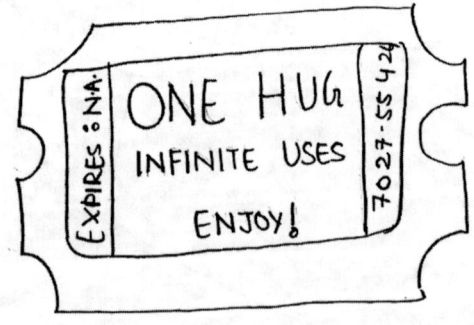

It all will make sense maybe
Not today,
Not tomorrow,
But one day,
The things which broke you
Will make sense.
And that
Will be the day of healing.

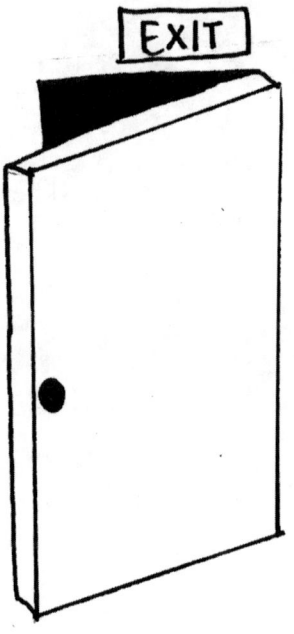

The hurt
Can never
Talk about love.
Ask the healed.
They know it the best

I need no reason
To be kind
And grateful

I need no reason
To smile at strangers
And tell a girl
That her hair is amazing.

I need no reason
To be happy or sad.
I don't have to attach
The strings
Of emotion and reason

If I feel something
My duty is to fully feel it
And not to ask
Why am I feeling this?

My duty is to
Let go of emotions
I don't want to feel
And not question them
Because
question marks at the end of sentences
Aren't that pretty to me.

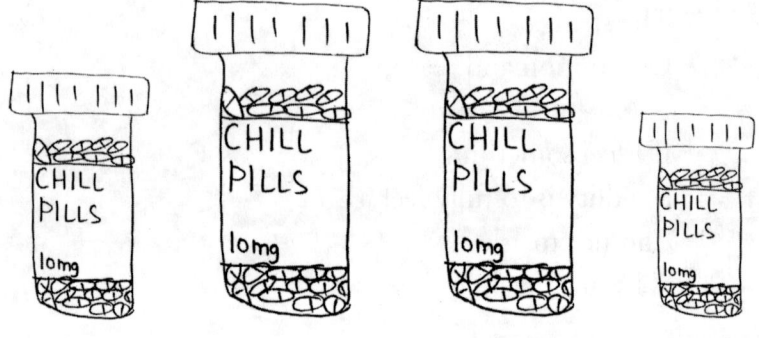

When
we were born
Our mothers never told us
That we are born for someone
They said
We are born for
Great things
&
I hope
No one ever forgets that.

This is
To all of us.
Because who hasn't been in love?
And when I say love
It is not your lover that
I am talking about It is all those other things
You have been in love with.
The moments,
The sunrises and sunsets,
The soil,
The moon,
Your pet,
Anything whom you gave your heart to.

for once
do it for your heart
and not for your body.
And watch it never leave you.

–the love

We don't need
The mouths
Who asks you,
"How are you?"
we need
Ears,
Who listen to Us
genuinely
When we answer
The above question.

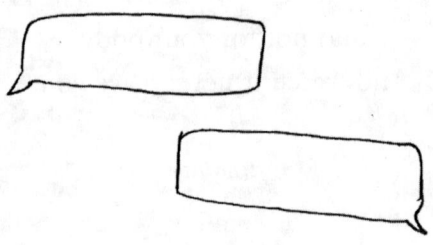

Take a break
Stop being available
For everyone
for a second.
 And be there for yourself
Fill the container
You've been
Endlessly pouring from.
You don't even realize
How many times
Your soul has cried your
name for help
And you were not there
To answer.
To help you.

You came with all
Miracles
Something
I might need
In the coming days
But
Not right now.

    —When the timing is wrong

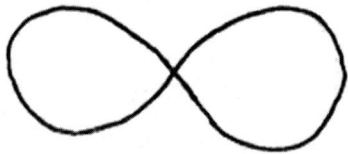

My lover
Is not supposed
To only take care of the heart
I gave him
He shall take care of my
Peace of mind as well
For if he thinks
It's only the heart
That I gave to him
He is all wrong.

—It's not only the heart that you give

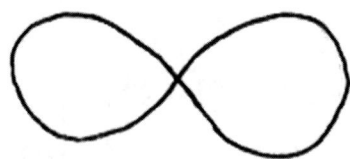

An old me
Is a difficult person
To make understand.
To persuade
To make see
All the harm
He has done to himself
But from here I see
& realize
He needs
All this breaking
To stand again
strongly and bravely
To stand the way
As if he does not know
What falling is.

You are such a bright diamond
That you don't fit
in any of the designs
this world has for you.
You,
on your own,
and all alone are the jewelry
The most beautiful
and the most expensive.
And if you know this about yourself
Then stop being in those hands
Which can not afford you.

    —My worth

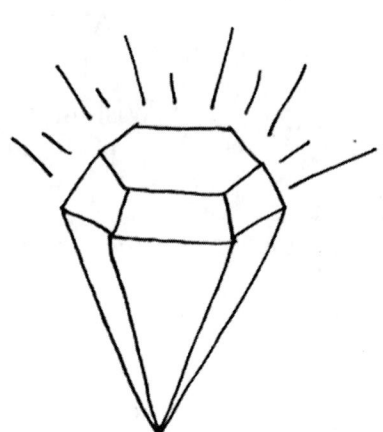

You have to believe
my love
whenever
I have closed my eyes
at 11;11
to wish for something
it was
always about you.
All the eyelashes
I have blown
Wishing for something
It was all for you.

—A *Love so selfless that I don't even wish for myself anymore*

Here I stand on the
Top of the mountains
Of my memories
I have created.
Looking and reflecting
Back at the life
That I have lived
As I go through the pages of
Book I have written
Or people I have met
Emotions that I have felt
And bad days that I have dealt
As I go through
The photographs
I want to keep
Of sometimes me laughing
On the top of my lungs
And sometimes
Of crying my eyes out
As I go through
The vague first's of my life.

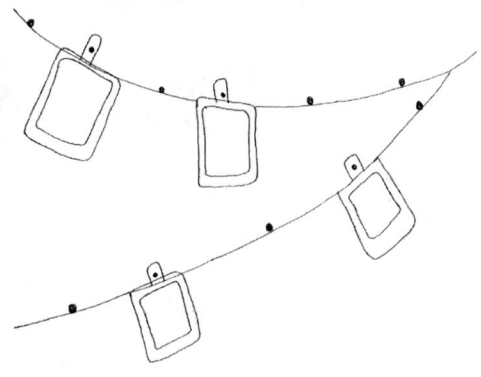

Yellow

The first time
I grew up
Or when I fell
In love.
The first day
I got a new perspective
Or the first day when I realized
I love the moon.
The first day
I moved onto
Better things
And
The first day
After which everything
Seemed normal
Here I stand on the
Mountain
Thinking how unappreciated
The first times are.

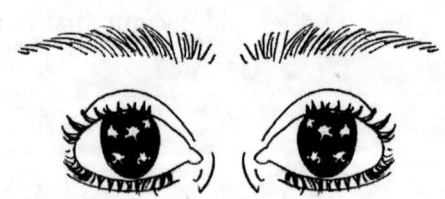

Thank you
Thank you so much
This is all I want to say,
For the closure.
I now go early from office
Some days
To have dates with me.
To cook my favourite meal
And have long showers
I now buy flowers
For myself
Since you have left
I have been there for me
A little more lately.

I grew up
Looking at the
Sunsets and
The sunrises
How can I not believe
In beautiful endings
And hopeful
Beginnings.

—better tomorrows

For me
today's goal
was to get out of my bed
 and see the sun rising.
 yesterday it was
to spend the entire evening
without having a breakdown
day before yesterday was
 to just smile at myself.
it is not always the goals
that define the meaning of life
or doing well in life
which keeps me going.
These little beads
make my necklace.

—It's okay

It doesn't have to be a big win
for me
to appreciate
myself.
the small battles
and war
I conquer daily
deserve my appreciation
and love as well.
For every drop
That contributes in building
The ocean,
Counts.

Universe sends
Hurting
And then it sends healing.
Just like
It sends rain
After a hot day
So what
If they injure you,
The one with the bandages
Is on his way.

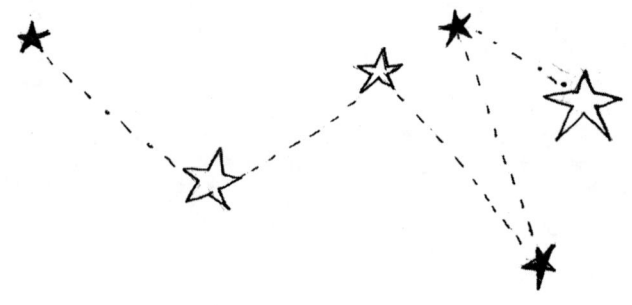

The new me
Is made of
Your absence
A lot of hope,
Happiness
And all those
Pieces of mine
I lost to you.

To all the women,
There are no doubts
That you deserve
The world
And it's greatness
But
Let's not forget that
So do they.

—men

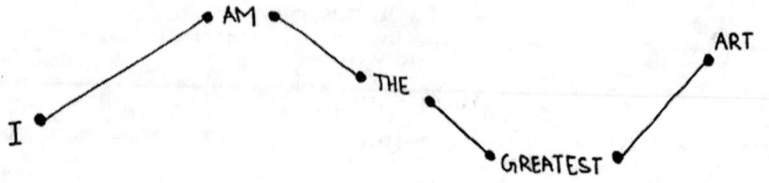

If the greatest artists
Of the universe
Came together
To birth one art.
That masterpiece
Would look like You.
Exactly like you.

—To me.

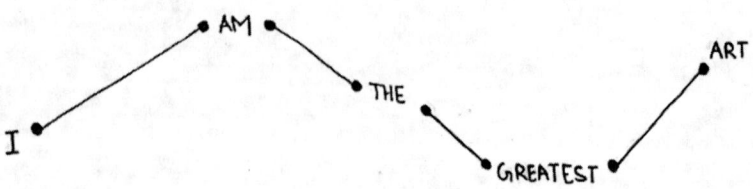

I was handed over
A list of people
Whom
I am supposed to make happy
And guess what
The first person
On that list Was myself.
And there was no second person on it
The world was never on the list.

—Do it for yourself

The biggest mistake
Is to address
Someone
As your first love
When you know
That it is nobody else
But
You, and yourself.

The biggest mistake
Is to promise them
That you will make them happy
When you haven't
Made yourself happy
Since years.

The biggest mistake
Includes
to promise
Someone that
You can't live your life
Without them
When you know
That no matter how much it pains
You will heal one day
And get over it.

The biggest mistake
Is to call everyone
Out there beautiful
And failing
To recognize
Your own beauty.

& if life gives
You a chance to amend
All these mistakes.
The biggest mistake
Is to let go
Of this opportunity.

I am writing letters
To the young women.
I am writing
All those things
that this society tried to teach me
Things my mother made me learn
Because she was made to learn them
By her mother.

All those norms,
And how my clothes determine
How safe I am in the world
That lies outside my home.
All those regulations.
Which made no sense to me,
Because they existed only for me
And not the males
I went to school with.

I am writing letters
To the young women. I am writing
That don't learn it
If it doesn't make sense to you too.

Don't change yourself
Because
It's my responsibility
To make the place safer
And not
Tell you to be careful.
For I can not ignore the
Broken road
And put a board
"be careful!" right next to it.

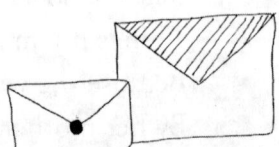

And now
I am writing
Letters to young men
 Because its time
For you to learn the norms
 And not the other gender.

And as I finish
I would like to tell
All of you
That
No one is less
Be it men, women or others
And no one's existence
Should be the reason
For other's pain.

So I asked my heart
Don't you miss him?
"I do!
I do miss him
When you are sitting
All alone by the fireplace

I miss him
When you get a good news
And the first person on your mind
Is him.

I miss him
When you almost-dial
His number
To ask what he would like to have
for dinner.

But I don't remember
His existence
When you stand in front of
Mirror & embrace
The masterpiece in you,
That the pain helped you become
I do not miss him
When you stand with the
Others of your tribe
Empowering them
To become their best.

It looks like
He never happened to you
When I see the kind
Of contribution he made
To the kind of
Woman you are
And you
Shall become."

—From the healed heart

To be honest
When I sit to write
About love and healing
I only realize, that
There is so much to be written about
And so less paper
To be written on.
So much less ink in this world
To be written from.

As much as I would like to say
That
you deserve the world
I rather choose to speak
That
this world deserves you.

—Your goodness and your kindness Along with
All your glories
The world deserves to see it all.

Tell me now
When I say love
Whose face appears in front of your eyes?
Now tell me
Is it yours?
Tell me now
Whose eyes you think of
When I say,
the most beautiful eyes,
Is it yours?
when I ask you
to think of the most lovable
Voice you've ever heard
Is it yours?
So tell me now how
often you've associated
The idea of being beautiful
with others And not you

I Let no one Tell me
That they are
My good days.
I remember
What it was like
When someone said it to me
the
Last time.

I owe myself a lot
The biggest apology
The greatest love
The major gratitude
I owe myself
All the happiness
I lost to the world.

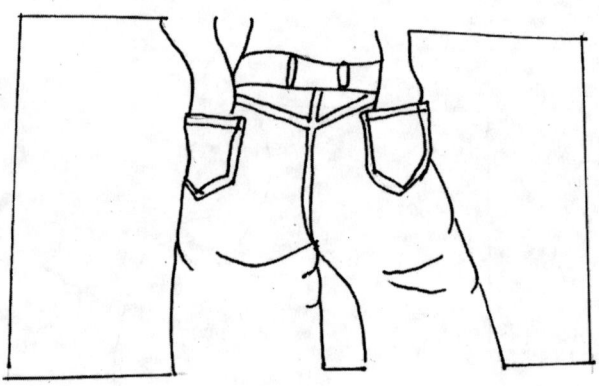

If you find
That it is
Your world which is
Falling apart
Let it.
And once it is shattered completely
Pick up the pieces
And build a crown out of it.
You own your
Broken parts.

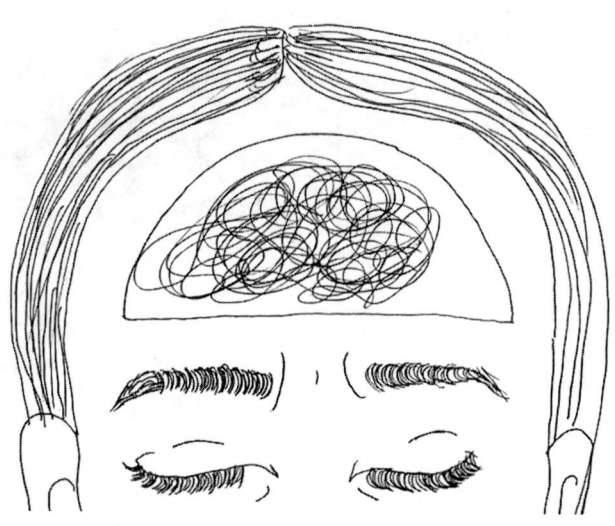

I press
My undereyes
I stop my tears
From coming out
I order them, 'FREEZE!' Come out
For the right one
I'll let you flow
When the person
Standing in front of me.
Will be worth it.
For now
Stay beneath me.
And I am sorry
That I am being so strict
But that's because
I know
That I won't learn easy

A consent slip
Requires my signature,
It is a permission
That I have to grant
Myself to heal
By signing it
I allow myself to heal
To change all those habits of mine
Which let people walk over me
To let go of those memories
Of ghosting at 2:00 am
And tell me
I am good for nothing.
But to sign it
Requires great courage
Probably
A very brave thing to do
Shall I ?

—Do you allow yourself to heal?

Yesterday,
I found her
The one,
who was lost
She was sitting in a garden
Surrounded by Doubts, grief, depression
And abandonment
I walked up to her
And took her by hand
Out of circle
I led the way
I showed her the light
The path
Yesterday, I found myself
The part who was lost

> *—only I can guide
> me out of this*

If Letting go
Is so hard
Then think of it
As an important decision
Either you can
Have them
Or
You can have yourself
Make the choice
And let one of them go.

Was I Supposed to go slow
So that
This would have
Lasted forever.
Should I have Cared less
Or cared not at all?
Should I have
Told you that
I love you
A bit less
So that its value
Remained preserved forever?
Should I have waited?
Before I confessed
To see
If you felt the same?
Did all this happen too soon?
We both did not know
When to stop
I was too soon to fall in love
And you were
Too soon to walk away.

  —What is the right pace?

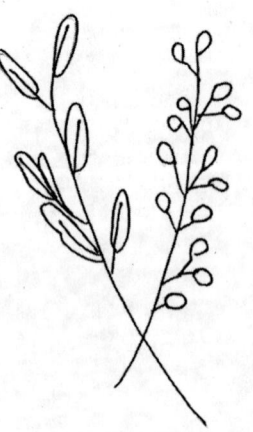

I wish
when you read this
You think of those people
Who broke you.
And realize,
it was never them
But you, yourself.
I wish,
you become aware
Of the healing, coming your way.
I wish,
you have this epiphany
That,
you
are your hurting and healing both.

One person
Writes about his heartbreak
And all other billions of people
Feel it
Why?
Because love is surely
A tricky thing
It robs all of us
In the same way.
And then
All that remains
Is the poems
And art
We all relate to.

He?
Oh no,
He is not a human
He surely is a God
For
all those millions of people
Who put their
Trust and faith
in God
I alone put that much believe
In him.

I am wise enough
To understand
That
The world is a circle &
The hate that I give
Will find its way
To me
One day for sure.
And human enough
To not practice it
Even if I know
The consequence.

    —The human dumdness and tendencies

When I talk about the hurting
I am speaking the yellow of the autumn
 When I say healing
I am thinking of the yellow of the spring.
Only yellow is both.

   —Why yellow?

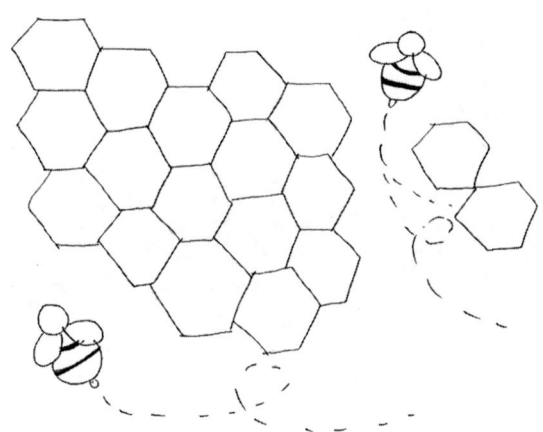

The ocean
shall remember
That if
he is not willing
To give a drop of water
To the river
Which has dried
Which is begging.
Then one day
He shall be prepared
To beg to the clouds
Who will not
Rain on him.
Despite of crying
And begging
Nothing will be given.

   –*Karma*

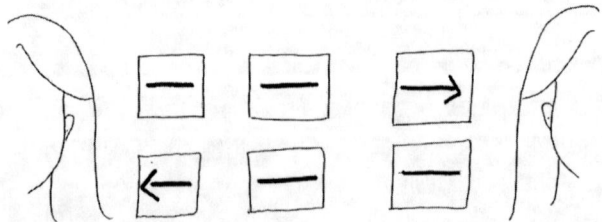

My sad moment
Is a dot
In this
Big book of life
And I am the writer
Determined to write So
One sad dot
And I close the book?
How is that
A wise decision

   –sucidal

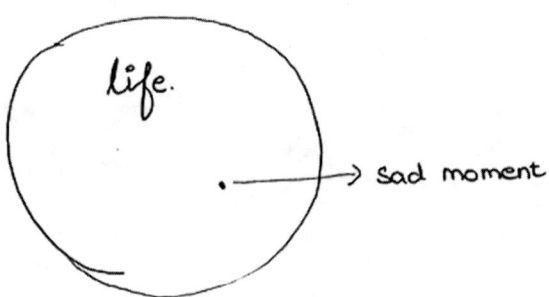

I don't remember
The book of love
That said,'
women
are supposed to love
Only men.
Your soulmate
Is not always
From the opposite gender.
Because
Why will
the gender bother you At all?
If it's their arms
Which feel like home.

–Pride

To love again
you will have to heal
because to love
with a heart
which is broken is like
giving pieces
of yours.
When
They deserve it all
A love in full.

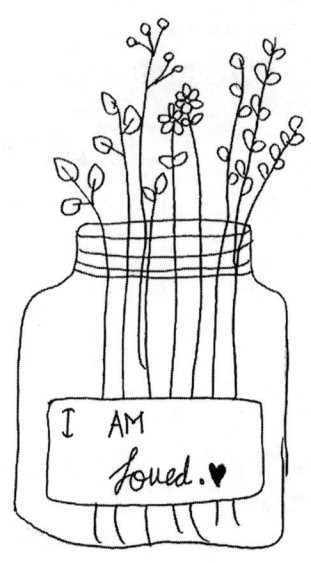

I want to go there
Where
My breath runs free
In the air
My voice touches the sky
And comes back
In my body.
I want to go there
Where even if
I roam uncovered
People don't think
It is a consent
To enter in my territory
where
There is no room for the judgement
Neither from any women
Nor men
Or anyone

–*The land of my dreams*

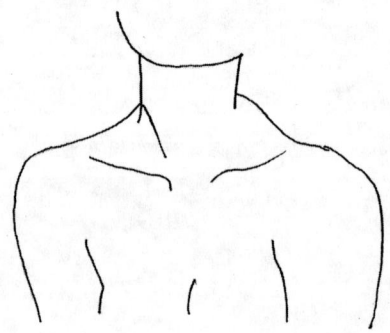

Every time
When I say
"my second love"
I see the eyes
Are On me
With judgement
It is not something wrong,
not a sin
She is that person
Who restored my believe
In love
For the second time.
I can love again.

I don't know men
And masculinity
If I think
their Short hair
Their beard
Their muscular structure and their hoarse voice
Makes them different from females.
I don't know them
If I think the piercings on their body
Is not man enough
I don't know them
If I think that they aren't supposed
To wear makeup
They aren't supposed to cry
And they aren't allowed to be sensitive.
and
Perhaps if I don't know men then
I don't know art.

Here,
I give you a list
Of all those things Which are okay
In the process of healing
Number one
It is okay for you to think that you've moved on
Yet still feel overwhelmed
When you think about them.
Number two
It is okay to have breakdowns
Which will convince you
That you haven't done enough but
Trust me
You will get past it.

Number three
It is okay
If you feel
That nobody will ever fill your heart with love
Just like they did
but
Someone will.
Number four
It is okay
To have no motivation to wake up in the morning
But that doesn't mean
You haven't progressed?

Number five
It is okay to feel
Everything is shit because
Everything will make sense to you soon
Number five
It is okay
To not socialize and to not be productive
If you need a break
Take it
There is nothing to be apologetic about.
And
It is okay
To feel
That you will never
Heal again
To look at your wounds and think
They will bleed forever
Take the last piece of trust
Left in you
And keep it for yourself
You will,
Every part of you
Will heal.

   –Healing

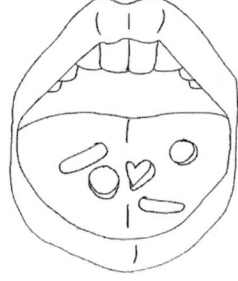

My vagina Makes me female.
It is my sexuality.
My act of standing with others like me
Makes me a woman.
On weekends when I am out
Eating dinner With other males When I stop to
notice If they only respect me Because they know
me But also all the other Women in the room
With unknown faces.
Maybe I am in the process,maybe I am already
there. But to call myself one without acting like her
Is the sin.
To not stand for my sisters around the world.
To talk of equality and integrity and myself harass
the rights of them.
I am not enough woman, if my morals who belittle
men are the ones on which I stand on.
I am not a woman if I don't make peace with all
other genders who exist.
I am not a woman if I molest other's rights to
enhance my own.
I am not a womanIf for me being a feminist means
Being anti-men.

   –The women I am becoming

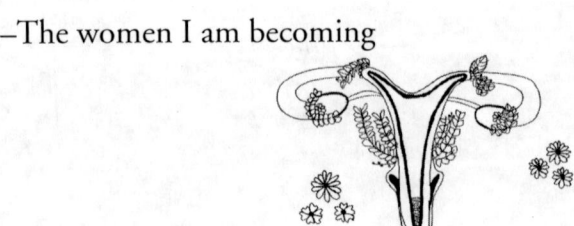

To close the eyes
And forget The pain
They caused you
Is not the thing
Doesn't make any difference.
For what is forgotten
Can be remembered again
So give it time
And let it heal
Let it be forgiven
Because
The forgotten can be remembered again
but the one
who is healed
Can never be hurt again.

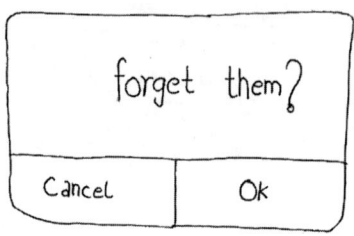

When I say
Long hair Piercings
Make up
Smooth skin
And
someone crying I don't know why
But you immediately think of women.
And when
I say RAPE
You immediately
Turn to men.

    —Gender norms.

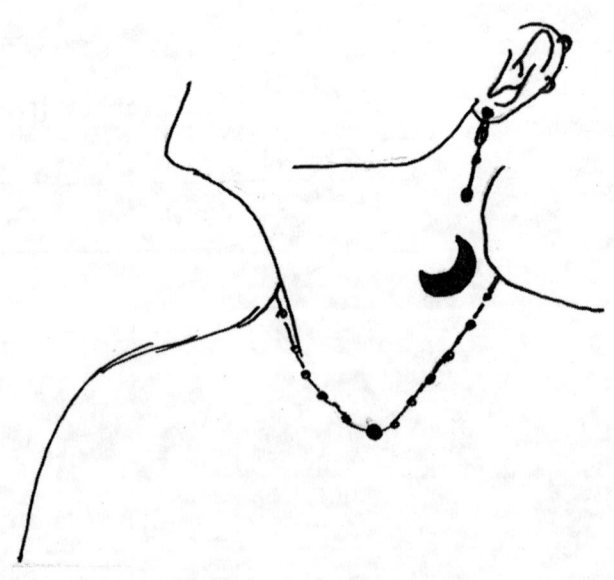

If
you will ask me
Who do I want to be like?
It's quiet a possibility
That I will not take a human's name
I want to be
Like the moon
In all its phases
She is beautiful
And appreciated
It doesn't have to be full
Or complete
To be loved by others
Whether she is Half, crescent
Or not there at all
It is always looked at
Waited for
I want to be like the moon.

One stretch mark
And you rush to cover it up
Then you see five more
And then you begin to see
All those things
Which you think should not be visible
Your lines on the face
And the cellulite on thighs
The wrinkles around your eyes
And the nails you wish were longer.
But
From rejection comes rejection
You reject one thing about yourself
And slowly you reject everything
And now from head to toe
You like nothing about yourself.
But Here is a spoiler
So comes the acceptance from acceptance
You accept one of your flaws
And suddenly you find everything about yourself
Beautiful.
Because if your body
Makes sense to you
It does not have to make sense
To anyone else
Out there.

  –Body positivity

To let go of them
Is not to
Only let go of their
Image in your head
It is to move on
From their every little thing
To forget
From their favourite color
To what they liked to have for their breakfast
It is to let go
Of your urge
To re check
Endless times
What they are posting
It is
To teach yourself no matter how hard it it
To not speak their name
Frequently
It is to not
Compare your every date
With the romantic dates you had with them
Letting go is
To accept
That life goes on
With or without them.

And maybe many people
Will come and go
And till the time
That one person arrives
To stay forever,
You have only yourself.

I am so healed
That neither
I remember the hurt
That has ever happened
Nor will I remember
The hurt
That will ever come my way
I have healed altogether
For the past
And for the future.
So all those
Who think
They can upset me again
Can find a new business to run.

The heart.
It never stops beating
Yesterday
It was, for them
Today, for me

   —Life goes on

Now that I have
Let go of this feeling
Of what it is like
To have a man on your body
Without you willing for it
I will make sure
No other female has to struggle with it again
I will make sure they dress
The way they want to
I will make sure
They enjoy themselves and have drinks if they want to
I will make sure
I correct the right part of society
And it's not the victim
Not the females
But the boys
I will make sure
They know what is the meaning of the word NO
I will make sure they know
It means to stop
To not touch

And be respectful.
I will make sure they know what it is like
To have that experience
And I will make sure
The males know that
It can happen to them as well
And that
Women are not born for it
And men are not safe
Either.

—Rape is unisexual and nobody deserves it.

Urja Joshi

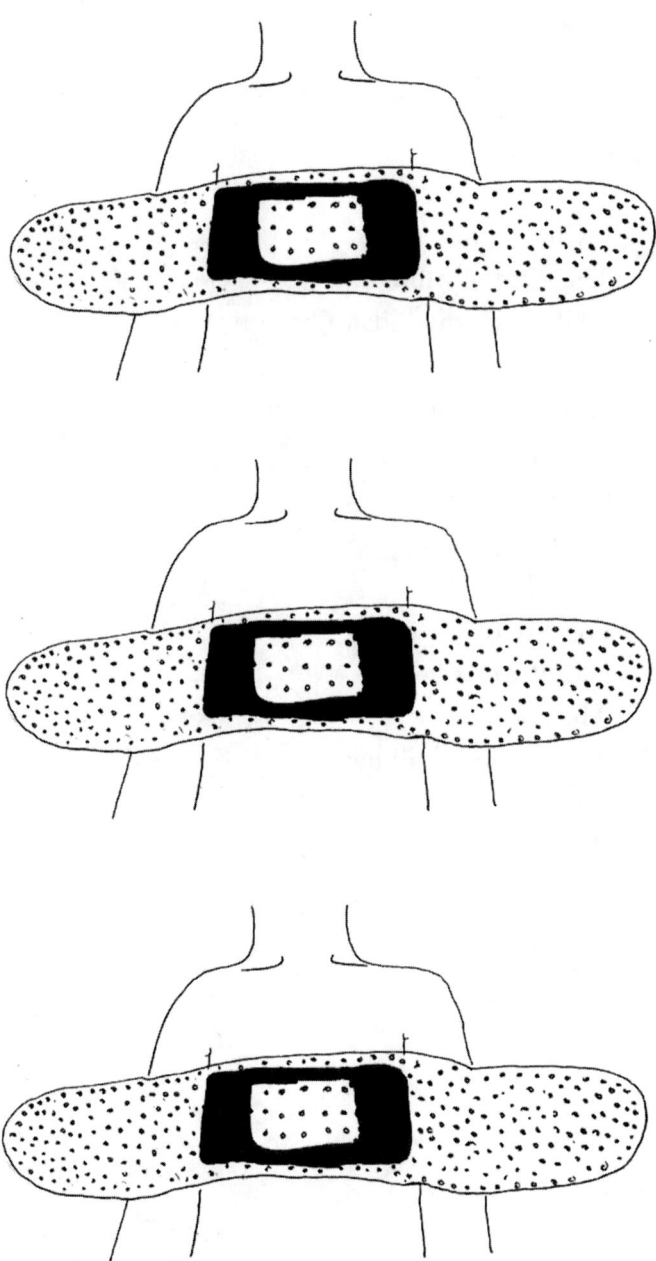

I want to see
What kind of
A person
I will evolve into
The kind of human
I will become
The kind of human
I will teach my kids to become
And the kind of
Human that will attract me
In future
I want to see
What will be my type
After 10 years
From here.
I want to see
The ending
This journey will have

And all these worries
Of tomorrows
Makes me forget
That today is the day
I wanted to see the yesterday.
And now today when
I am worrying about
The day to come
I shall remember
That when the day
Finally comes
I will be busy worrying about
The coming one.

  —When will I really enjoy?

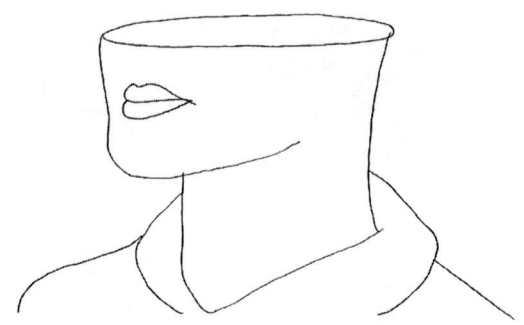

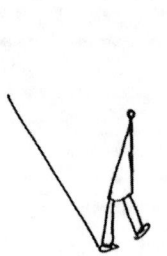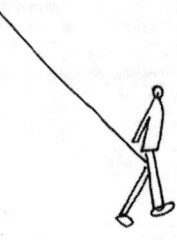

Our meeting
Was a faint line
Between coincidence and destiny.
I don't know
If we just ran into each other
Or if every single event in my life
Has led me to you.

I wanted to be so many things
But out of all
I wanted to be my own audience
For once
I wanted to do
Everything
For myself
Just for me to watch.

Silence would make me so uncomfortable
But with you
Silence was justA type of conversation
We had with our lips closed
And tongues unmoved
I could listen to you
Even when you were just breathing

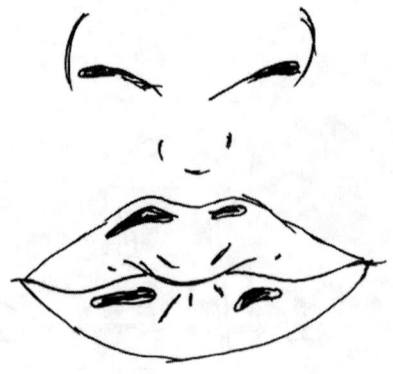

Of Course you're in discomfort,
You are leaving behind
What you wanted
And moving towards
What you need.

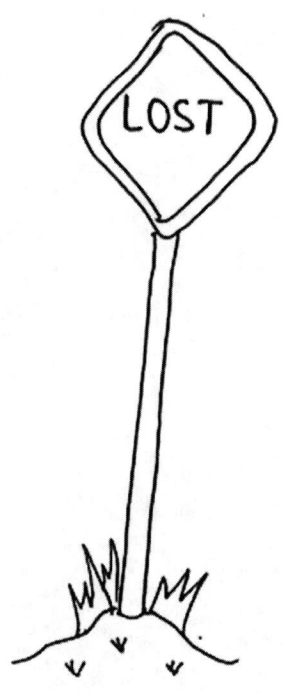

I hope I see you again someday and
I hope that when I do
I am able to smile my brightest
And thank you with every bone in my body
"Thankyou for walking away from me,
so that I could walk back home to myself."

Archived!
All the letters
We should have
Written
To ourselves.

The letter of apology

I collect all the sorry's
I have
given to this world
And
Give
All of them
To myself.
–I am sorry, me

Read it when you feel you have had enough

Dear YOU,

I am starting this letter with the word "irony". The human irony is that we all have so many intense emotions in us, be it love, or the guilt, the rage or the aggression. We have always felt that for others, our emotions come rushing into us, whenever it is associated with other people like us.

The love? For others, anger? For others The pity? For others

And today such are the emotions in me. I feel guilty. A guilt of loving everyone on this earth but myself.

I have loved the most unnecessary things and people in my life, only if I knew that the love I throw to everyone is something, which I needed the most.

My love is mine first and then others. I have the most right on it. I don't feel sorry for realizing it late because to have a late realization is better than not having it, at all.

Hence, I apologize to myself for not being there for me.

I apologize for often taking the path that I knew will take me farther away from my own self. I am sorry that I let people abandon me and then hurt my own self.

I apologize for setting the bar of expectations from others, way too high and too low for the expectations I had from myself. I apologize for every night I have spent crying and not doing the thing that made me the happiest.

I am sorry for not wearing colors that filled me with happiness and rather wearing what others liked or cherished. I am sorry for letting people break me and for thinking that they decide my strength.

I am sorry for not being strong enough and taking charge of myself.

I am sorry for taking so much care of others that I forgot to do that for me. And with this, I know I am forgiven because you are very kind.

All the love in my heart and all the other parts of me, is dedicated to you.

I am on the path to give you everything that I owe to you and everything that you deserve.

Always and only yours
You (but wiser)

The letter of hope
*Read it when you feel nothing will be right
Ever again.*

Dear YOU,

To say that I am thankful for everything that you have done for me, will be an understatement. I start this letter by just telling you how great of a human being you are. To find the good in people, even in the face of all the negativity they may display; to derive joy from others' happiness, despite knowing they may not be there to celebrate your own; to love and give endlessly to someone when there may be no expectation of reciprocity. It all takes so much strength which cannot be imagined, even in the most unreal imaginations. How beautiful it is to see you not losing hope and faith in the world's goodness after encountering every possible hurdle you could. I am not the creator nor a destroyer, I am a human and to promise you that something good is going to happen to you will not be so true. But I am you, all the hope that you have inside you, resides in me as well. That's why with all this light inside me I assure you that all the goodness that you offer to this world will one day make their way back to you.
All the thank yous and gifts, all the love and sorrys that you have given to this world with or without any reason will come back to you for sure.
One day you will find someone who will have the eyes to look beyond your imperfections and will have the heart who will hold oceans and oceans of

love and patience for you. And even till the day of final judgement, those oceans will not dry up. You will find someone who will be whole and will make you realize your own completeness as well. Who will make you realize that no other man completes you. You are not broken and you are not finding a person who can fit you well, he will make you realize that you are complete on your own. And that someone will make you the happiest.

And no this is not over expecting from life, because look at you, look at all that you have given to all of them, the ones who were right but just not right enough for you. Look at all that you have given to the people around you, look at all the moments where you have been extremely selfless.

And when you cherish it all, tell me don't you think that you deserve it? Don't you think it is not over expecting but to be honest the basics you can ask for.

Let the world think that it is too much for you, all the happiness, the glorifying success, all the great things but don't team up with the world and think that too. Don't say that it is too much for you. For if you think that way the universe will take all that back from you.

You don't need this hope and letter because you are the source itself. But I wanted to write anyway because I know you have listened all those things that I have thrown at you, maybe in frustration or

rage Or maybe all those times when I did not feel good enough. Here I am amending all of that and telling you all that you really are and all that you really deserve to listen to.
All the love inside my heart to you.

Mine and mine
You (but wiser)

The letter of love
*Read it anytime, because you
deserve love from yourself
more than love from anyone else.*

Dear you,

The eyes that take my breath away and the sound that is the melodious music in my ears, the face which makes me wonder how beautiful one can be. It is no one else's but yours. You spend a lot of time thinking why aren't you gorgeous like others or the other person?

Why aren't your hair thicker, skin fairer, voice sweeter, eyebrows more visible, breasts perkier, legs taller? I am here to tell you that you are the most beautiful human I have ever laid my eyes on and you are not gorgeous like them, because you are gorgeous like you. I know that some days it's not enough to listen that only I adore you, some days you want to hear it from others, somedays you want others to tell you that you are beautiful and you take their breath away but it's okay if they fail to tell you this thing. Because if some day you are not the world's definition of beautiful then it is not a big deal. You are your own type and that is enough. I love everything and every detail about you

How much you care for those people who step on you again and again and yet you choose to see the best in them. No matter how brutally uncomforting things you have heard yet you always have the most patient ear to lend to people. How kind you are to give those pieces and parts of yours to the world with full awareness that you will never get anything like that in return.

And as I am in awe of you, I continue writing this letter to you because if nobody has told you yet that you are a masterpiece then here it is me writing that about you.

The universe created you and then was so proud of you that it smiled at you and then filled you with all her greatness. The love you carry for others is your strength don't let the people tell you that you are a fool for believing the wrong ones. For a person like you there is nobody wrong and nobody right, your love is beyond everything. And I am here to tell you that if you have any of the slightest idea of the power of love you carry within you, then please give a fraction of it to yourself.

I am here to ask you if you accept me and cherish me. I am here to tell you if you want to spend the rest of your life with me because before you go and ask somebody else to be with you forever, do you want to be with yourself forever?

Do you want to spend your life with yourself?

Doesn't matter how many people have broken you and damaged you. Doesn't matter how many times you have been played with and walked upon. The only thing that matters is that despite all of it,

You stand here;

Grown and healed, your power is unfathomable and you I don't have words for that.

I love you
Haven't said it enough. But yes
I love you,
And I mean it.
I mean it more than
I have ever meant it for someone.

Mine and mine
You (but wiser)

The letter of gratitude
Because you were there for yourself
When nobody else was.

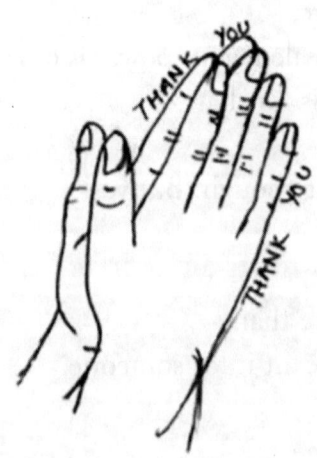

Dear You,

When I search through the memories that I've made, I can't even find one, where I am thanking you for coming so far with me on this journey, which has been filled with both highs & lows, a journey which has been a combination of some of the best days of my life and then days which I never thought I'd survive.

Every Time I've felt alone in the darkness of my head, I always found you by my side when I had no one by my side, I was never truly lonely, because I had you. You've seen every version of me, the versions that I've discarded, the versions I am still developing and the versions that may come up in future, you've loved me through it all.

You watched me, when I believed that some other breathing human could be my home, you watched me when the feeling of home in others often betrayed me and I returned to you, and promised you that I'll never go to some other person again in the search of love, you watched me break my promises and do it all over again, you watched me make some of the most terrible mistakes of my life, which costed me my peace, sanity and respect, you watched me watch people leave everything I offered to go in search for something better.

but most importantly you watched me come back home to you, even after a thousand disappointments, you always opened the door for me, and welcomed me back with a warm blanket. You reminded me that the only constant thing about this forever changing world is you, or in other words, "me". You reminded me that people leave, and there is good in goodbyes, that it's okay for some endings to never make sense and it's okay to walk out of it even when you promised them a forever, because your heart doesn't feel safe with them.

You were there for me in all the seasons of life, you held my hand when the strong winds of grief hit us, and when the roof of self confidence and esteem came shattering down upon us. Is a thank you, an understatement? For everything you've done for me. When what I feel for you is so much greater than the feeling of gratitude.

Your presence and the love that you offer me is so great that I wonder if anyone outside this body will ever love me like you do. It's because of you that I know what truly, true love is, what it truly means to be invested in someone, unconditionally. Thankyou with every beat in my heart, bone in my body, thought in my head, for being here with me, even when I thought I'd never know warmth again.

You make every harsh cold day of January feel like the sun is shining just on my face in July. You make me feel like someone has my back even when everyone has turned theirs on me.

You make my life worth living everyday and I wonder if I can say something greater and more meaningful than just a THANK YOU.

Because all that you do for me, is so much more than I ever expected anyone to do for me.

I hope every time in life, when I lose my way, when I lose people, when I run out of excuses to defend myself,

you're there to save me, I hope every time I take longer than usual to return home to myself, you wait for me by the door and smile when you see me coming.
I only want you to open the door for me.

Mine and mine
You (but wiser)

Acknowledgements

The masterpiece comes to an end, and how can this book end without this page of my respect and the gratitude towards people who truly made this possible..

I am truly blessed to have the support and love of so many people in my life and in everything I choose to do. My parents, I love you mom and dad, thank you so much for everything and for this beautiful life.

Thank you Aastha, my little sister for being such an honest critic and a true partner in crime, you make everything so much better. My little pet LEO, thank you for always cheering me up by licking my face, you're truly my child.

A big big big thanks to my publishing team and Sagar sir, for helping me in bringing my vision to life, for always letting me be playful and creative with my project. I am so grateful to everyone at Anecdote Publishing House for helping me with my creation. A big shoutout to my cover designer for getting the job done in the best way possible.

I want to take a moment and thank all of my friends. I don't know what I would have done without you guys and you all know who you are. Thank you to all those who make my life better by just being in it.

Thank you so much universe for this unbelievable manifestation of my dream, you know that there is no one I am more grateful to, than you.

The love of my life, my readers, thank you so much you lovely souls for making this compilation of art , a book. I love you guys, thank you so much. It's because of you that I write and that I'll continue to write.

I believe everything in this universe chooses its destiny, thank you so much yellow for choosing to be written by me, thank you for letting me be your birth giver.

Ending this, by expressing my gratitude towards the woman I transformed into by the time this project came to an end. I'm so proud of her and so happy to be her.

Thank you thank you thank you
By Yours truly
Urja

*I AM HEALED.
AND NOW
I TAKE BACK,
ALL THE RIGHTS FROM THIS WORLD
TO EVER HURT ME
AGAIN.*

This is the beginning of the beautiful yellows in your life. Spring is here.
The season of grief Has passed.
Let's welcome it
    —From mohi and kabir